The Room Where I Was Born

The Brittingham Prize in Poetry
The University of Wisconsin Press Poetry Series
Ronald Wallace, General Editor

Places/Everyone • Jim Daniels
C. K. Williams, Judge, 1985

Talking to Strangers • Patricia Dobler
Maxine Kumin, Judge, 1986

Saving the Young Men of Vienna • David Kirby
Mona Van Duyn, Judge, 1987

Pocket Sundial • Lisa Zeidner
Charles Wright, Judge, 1988

Slow Joy • Stephanie Marlis
Gerald Stern, Judge, 1989

Level Green • Judith Vollmer
Mary Oliver, Judge, 1990

Salt • Renée Ashley
Donald Finkel, Judge, 1991

Sweet Ruin • Tony Hoagland
Donald Justice, Judge, 1992

The Red Virgin: A Poem of Simone Weil • Stephanie Strickland
Lisel Mueller, Judge, 1993

The Unbeliever • Lisa Lewis
Henry Taylor, Judge, 1994

Old and New Testaments • Lynn Powell
Carolyn Kizer, Judge, 1995

Brief Landing on the Earth's Surface • Juanita Brunk
Philip Levine, Judge, 1996

And Her Soul Out Of Nothing • Olena Kalytiak Davis
Rita Dove, Judge, 1997

Bardo • Suzanne Paola
Donald Hall, Judge, 1998

A Field Guide to the Heavens • Frank X. Gaspar
Robert Bly, Judge, 1999

A Path Between Houses • Greg Rappleye
Alicia Ostriker, Judge, 2000

Horizon Note • Robin Behn
Mark Doty, Judge, 2001

Acts of Contortion: A Book of Poems • Anna George Meek
Edward Hirsch, Judge, 2002

The Room Where I Was Born • Brian Teare
Kelly Cherry, Judge, 2003

The Room Where I Was Born

Brian Teare

THE
UNIVERSITY OF
WISCONSIN PRESS

The University of Wisconsin Press
1930 Monroe Street, 3rd Floor
Madison, Wisconsin 53711- 2059
uwpress.wisc .edu

3 Henrietta Street
London WC2E 8LU, England
eurospanbookstore .com

Text and cover design by Mira Nenonen
Printed in the United States of America

Library of Congress Cataloging-in-Publication Data

Teare, Brian.
The room where I was born / Brian Teare.
pp.   cm.—(The Brittingham prize in poetry)
ISBN 0-299-19400-0 (hardcover: alk. paper)—
ISBN 0-299-19404-3 (pbk.: alk. paper)
I. Title. II. Brittingham prize in poetry (Series)
    PS3620.E427 R66   2004
  811'.6—dc21   2003006271

The poems in this book are acts of the imagination,
and the characters therein inventions. Neither poems nor
characters should be mistaken for reality, the context
that invents imagination.

ISBN 978-0-299-19403-1 (e-book)

I found him.
I held him and wouldn't let him go
 until I took him to my mother's house,
to the room where I was born.

—Song of Songs

Contents

II

Acknowledgments

These poems first appeared (sometimes in very different form) or are forthcoming in:

Campbell Corner Poetry Prizes: "Begin, Beware—"; *Columbia: A Journal of Literature and Art:* "Rules for the Telling"; *Connecticut Review:* "The room where I was born"; *Crazyhorse:* "Apiary"; *Fourteen Hills:* "'A Family Establishment'—"; *Gulf Coast:* "Because David and Jonathan"; *Meridian:* "Against Abstraction" and "Circa (I–IV)"; *Notre Dame Review:* "Begin, Beware—" and "Poem between Line Breaks"; *Painted Bride Quarterly:* "Dangerous Kitchen"; *Pleiades:* "Agoraphobia: A Reply" and "Sleeping Beauty and the Prince: Self-portrait as Victim & Perpetrator"; *Ploughshares:* "The Word Cock & the Sublime"; *Poet Lore:* "Tenement Body"; *Quarter After Eight:* "Bad like," "Children's Songs," "Marriage Elegy"; *Quarterly West:* "Then we were Raptured"; *Sonora Review:* "Trick Noir"; *Spoon River Poetry Review:* "First person plural is a house"; *Sundog: The Southeast Review:* "Detail from 'Set for a Southern Gothic,'" "Set for a Southern Gothic"; *Virginia Quarterly Review:* "House in Summer with a Slapped Face in It."

Many thanks to the dedicated staff and editors of the above journals and the readers who help them continue; Indiana and Stanford Universities for fellowships and teaching positions that gave the time, money, and communities that aided in the completion of these poems.

For my teachers who were kind enough to offer instruction, for those who read drafts, for indispensable help, editorial and otherwise, and/or for the gifts of friendship and kinship, artistic and otherwise: Aaron Baker, Rick Barot, Simeon Berry, John Paul Eakin, Eavan Boland, Gaby Calvocoressi, Julie Carr, Jen Chang, Josh Corey, Romayne Dorsey, Patty Lawson, Beach and Leeny MaloneBeach, Alyce Miller, Susan Mitchell, Cornelia Nixon, Z. Z. Packer, Angella Pneuman, Adrienne Rich, Lisa Spadafora, Maura Stanton, Jean Valentine, Kayoko Wakamatsu, Paul-Victor Winters, David Wojahn—and to Kelly Cherry, who believed in this book—to all of you: thanks are not enough.

For those stalwart, patient and loving souls—Margaret Ronda and Kerri Webster—who read and commented on as many as four drafts of this book: unending gratitude.

To Tom Haydon at Wessex Books—for two and a half years among lovers of books, and books, lots of, and to Sally-Ann—for kinship and cat-sitting.

Most of all, for beginning, thanks belong to my first teachers (Sheryl Cohen) for teaching the music, and (Thomas Rabbitt) for showing, by example, how deep it might run.

I

Circa

Say it was father bought the word and made it his with a picture:
   at first you'd think *summer*

the way light, like heat, supples roof and shutter with ripple, but,
   sun mirage or miracle,

it's his, he owns it now. Mother's camera cropped the shot;
   her body falls long upon a child

like shrubbery he's dug a joke shovel under to uproot, beware:
   beneath a mother's shadow

a boy grows crooked. Photo with no year, white child
   with no name: but I know

it's me young, perhaps even before words had grown adult,
   meaning like bones still soft

and accommodating, and the shape behind me not yet *house*,
   though soon enough it'd be

a noun as solid as a contract, as if two men shook over the good dirt
   of its name and one of them

built the thought inside it. Intrinsic as salt, aspirate—*h*\—
   so soft in mother's mouth

it laid a body down dreaming and rose up around that boy:
   house: a noun but with arms

inside. The story of family began where and when, what film
   coiled in what black canister,

negative frames' faceted patterns jeweled and taut as a snake's
   tensed back, in whose archival eye

do images now recoil and strike? \'haus\: that sibilant hiss haunts
   the end, word that began so soft

in memory of my mother's body and I would begin again—

After the thorns I came to the first page.

—Randall Jarrell

Rules for the Telling

Rules for the Telling

(after Jarrell)

Her telling has rules, the child knows, parts
as in a play: one who is voice, one who is ear;
stories happen forever just outside the wide skirt
of light. Far into that far-away, thorns clamber
the walls' rot, nine crows fuss, shake down their nests
in the closets' hats, nails wait in loose skeins of rust
beneath the milky surface of the bath, and hear?,
faintly now, an undercurrent—

                     other characters wait
as late inside this story the mother reads
her son fairy tales once read to her in German.
Her voice draws the limits of the late-night room—
wavering circle—her voice a wick burning inside
a cut-glass chimney filmed with oil and smoke,
channeling ash to the ceiling. In every telling:
a house neither voice nor ear must enter: a house
in which men who are not kings live. The size
and shape of that house is the size and shape of not-
telling, not-hearing: wood floors brittle, spark-prone
as flint, and the façade, sweet to look at, and light
as cheap cake.

           Everything depends upon upkeep,
the shape of that house; the poverty of telling
an ill-framed door that sticks, what it is to listen
is the walls' gaunt garden of ruined flowered paper:
everything depends on what waits just outside
the light, where the child thinks all stories happen.
Yes, there's smooth tangible black like asphalt,
a hundred roads out of rooms so precious they're held
in the hand, there, where her telling stops.

                                        But out past
the closets riffled with feathers, beyond the bath
in which nails bleed the water red, there, in the house
whose walls are not yet veined, trained to ruin
as the vines' frail, failing arbors, there—

                                the men dream of them.

These are the rules. Soon the walls will fold
into sepia rolls, and within deepening tint, the mother's
voice will dim, the telling lose its hold. . . . She must tell
each story as if it were otherwise. The child knows
when the book and voice and light give up and go
to bed under another name, nine crows will hatch,
spilling from hats as if from brown felt eggs, nails
will spin in their red watery beds, and the hundred roads
will fill with the sound of walking.

                        She will tell it—
what else can she do?—and the name of a man
who is not a king will pick the lock of the story
with a thorn, and, bed undone like a zipper,
the child will fall all night, and it will go unheard,
unpunished in the untold dark. I swear to you:
this is knowledge: the child awake as the light goes out.

First person plural is a house

where I put myself in third person in a bed I know
his older brother's hands will visit. It's no mistake incest starts

with an eye: at this distance they're theoretical as dolls, rhetorical
as pain imagined, but they can't see the word they create

with their bodies, can't know such bodies won't stop speaking,
always that word on the tongue in the mouth of another.

In the kitchen stands Mother, wringing her hands,
wet laundry: no: rubbing their stained fabric together

to clean them of song. Living room geometry: Father's face acute;
a bottle of whiskey: his arithmetic kisses. How many fingers, sucked

down, will fill him? How many until the bottle's clear?
On the porch, outside the poem, I smoke a cigarette, note

how a narrative's ending denotes another beginning, how
no bottle remains empty, no hands, no mouth or hips. I'm not worried;

no one else watches his story being written. I want to know:
with what grammar he'll enact it, with which line, breaking,

he'll hold the slip of syntax between him
and me. When I say "I" I mean eye, sum of my watching.

Sleeping Beauty & the Prince:
Self-portrait as
Victim & Perpetrator

Yes, it's a joke—in the florists' dictionary,
    a deep burgundy rose means
        unconscious beauty.

If withered and white, the bud's irony
    has two meanings—*fleeting beauty*
        & *you made no impression*—as in
            the first story: I wake

fucked. Or version 2: centuries pass.
    The witch doctored me a curse
        to marry marry marry and while I sleep,
            she deals me nomenclature
                from her book of roses—

Solitude/Paradise/Crystalline Secret Moonstone—
    the sweet, sugary names of my own incipient damp,
        her numens to combat its fever and heat.

It's true, you can't be too careful—every virgin holds a yes,
    those lips, a hothouse flower. A young rose opened
        in full and placed over the tight purses of two new buds
            drives a girl to heat and secrecy . . .

So then he wakes me with that coy prick—
    sibling kiss—lips shorn of bramble
        and sex. Henceforth, Ever-After means
            after marriage.

Yes: please, let's rather have the first story:
    his lips soft as any closed petals'
        purse, my pulse
            surfaces raw roses
                trellised at the wrist.

Yes: a kiss. Yes: coaxes a slow
    clamor of color in my cheeks.
        Arbor of bones on which he grows,
            my sleep opens to his skin,
                limbs' slim vines.

Yes: my sex,
    nascent earth in which he thumbs deep—
        Timeless Shining Hour/ Pristine Perfect Moment/
        Bride's Dream—his roseate tongues,
            his flowery names.

What do I know of name, the thousand
    pretty ways to say Prince, only one
        of which is Brother? I've been asleep—
            how could I imagine such hands?

Poem between Line Breaks

[*Why?*]

So that after, every kiss could become metaphor, but a metaphor for what?

      [*The old one—his body*
      a house? His body of locked rooms
      and his brother inside?]

Okay. Here is the door—

      [*hollow, cheap pine*
      rickety with holes
      and how will it hold, how
      will it hold the telling—]

where the brother tests the knob

      [*(locked) and behind that,*
      the story
      where the boy looks up
      from this book]

as if his point of view could mean something here.

I give you the house—

      [*pink siding, blue shag rug*
      in the basement,
      wood paneling, mildew
      creeping through the grain—]

how pipes knock plaster loose in the ceiling.

I give you the brother,

> [*but not what leads him*
> *to crouch here. Tell me,*
> *what would move you*
> *most? Instinct? Gullet*
> *and hunger? A door*
> *he knows he could break?*]

And if I make him more than his actions,

> [*would it matter to you?*
> *What detail would move you*
> *more? "Out of his fourth institution*
> *in as many years" or*
> *"He's stopped taking Lithium*
> *because 'it' isn't the 'real' him"?*]

would you be able to see him?

I doubt anyone—the family, the boy—is able to *see* him

> [*except as "really sick,"*
> *or "a burden," as in—*
> Can we trust?
> What to do with?]

Does that change things?

I want to know

> [*what makes him*
> *make me tell*
> *this story, the one*
> *where I can't lie*]

no matter how improbable the outcome.

The boy being young, the brother drunk,

[*you must understand the first kiss*
does not begin here
so much as it grows in probability—]

The boy afraid—

[*the sound of the lock*
being picked, and air conducting
the shock, panic
prolonging the breakage. . .]

What happens next is easiest—

[*his brother fucking him*—]

afterward is more difficult.

There are many reasons for this.

[*The parents in the room*
above, not hearing
it happen, not making it real.]

Does that change things?

And what of that, the not-hearing?

[*Because before that no story,*
no metaphor, a body
a body, his brother
his brother. And even being fucked
just that: pain
predicated on correct grammar,
syntax: subject
verb object.]

And what of blame?

Who? With what syntax?

16

Perhaps you say that at a moment like this, it is not possible to think,

> [*and I say "Yes, true: tell me: who*
> *and how." Say "I said easiest,*
> *the boy never confused*
> *until after—the long not-hearing*
> *in which he will remember*

a kiss came to be

> *a house made real forever—*

his brother inside the room—

> *his body."]*

Begin, Beware—

Begin, Beware—

I.

—Invocation—

Begin sinister. Sincerity like a fairy tale, some treacle
    laced fatal with arsenic's false almond, but begin. Yes, tell us
        Once there was a boy who loved a story so much he walked through the page,

tell us how *There was white, rooms incendiary without shadow,*
    and even if you ask *How can you understand how it was, the others*
        calling him back, even if you give us *How the simple loop of O was a noose*

ready to choke, I a knife that splits, don't think we don't
    know already. Here, memory's every Once & Once & Once
        we ever heard—time's upon itself until the self's a strange,

a second person. Ruthless: museless: first person's worst
    inversion, a witch isn't bitch enough to do *you* justice.
        When you tell us *His lips were perfect of diction,* how, *Outside,*

the words sat black like birds, hooked beak and claw deep in glass,
    all along we've known *On the other side the other child waited,*
        the bad brother, how *The others sent him to fetch the boy back.*

And when he says, *"Dear Brother come, you've lost your name;*
    you must be cold without it," tell us everything the bad one
        wants, spare us nothing we don't already know, tell us

and your voice will alter with telling, gnarl and knot
    like bark: beware: a scar's the shape a song takes;
        any such singing leaves its mark. Yes, it's true *The boy knew a name*

is the largest bird, eyes cut cruel as obsidian, knew a name is hungry,
    a carrion keeper, but you will anyway, won't you, croon
        the catastrophic lyric, cream it, diva the infernal tessituras,

because it's aria, it's yours, opera written for the burning
        stage, & ah—you have to: this pit's literal. This is Hell:
                a tale's told & here remains forever. As if a teller's guilt

weren't punishment enough, when the bad one whispers,
        "Don't pretend you've forgotten how we slept tight as spoons, our skin
                fit over the bones of our name," when he says, *"You must be hungry;*

please, step closer: I've something for you," implore us, *Oh Reader,*
        a plum, and give us *Its color deep as the throat's hum and plush,* show us
                how *His hand reached through the glass*—and beware. We suffer forever

how our stories begin—

—In the Library of the Fairy Tale,

there's one the folklorists
catalog under the key-word *brothers*. In the *Thematic Index*

of Folk-Lore & Fairy Tale—the limbo where stories go—
the scholar's virtuosity is compression: figuration, essence,

all the blood and doves of Schwarzwald gone. No raconteur
could stand it—*extra-ordinary companions are* b.; *disenchantment*

by sewing shirt for enchanted b.; *magic object stolen by* b.; *b. having*
extra-ordinary skill—all the etceteras & excesses of oral tradition

pared to suggestion, fragment. You thought you might not
find your story after all in the Teller's Book, the entries sick

with benignities, all the awful plucky brothers playing nice-
nice, the blackbirds let loose from their blackbird pies . . .

But in someone's hand the wicked history is recorded—
b. *chosen rather than husband*; *lecherous* b.—perhaps an Archivist

of Harm, Indexer of Punishable Husbandry (old Latin story,
incestus, "impure": kiss stanched black as bad teeth, thrill

a vermilion risen at the root of the mouth, nervy as rills
& licks
        mockingbirds sing
           as shadows swing
       beneath the meat
          in the gallows-tree),

                & in what untraveled
backwater did he first hear the tale? In what sticky kitchen did he

listen as an old bachelor smoked, told the one that begins *Once*
upon a time, a brother loved his brother, the sorrow of all beginning:

impossible for a scholar to ascribe origin or author; no matter
how he came to learn it, the teller can only say, *Sir, it's always been*

a borrowed song.

—The Milk-Father

Once a young husband for a year grew restless
beside his wife & each night he left their bed
no one could say where he went. & when did it

begin, children saying a wolf without howl lived
in the wood, midnight bade stolen boys drink
from a row of swollen, hairless teats? *Boys grow old*

fast in these parts, mothers said, and witness-
less, the man famished the mouths of cradles,
milktooth and fatherbreast, false beast he took

the boys to him & together bred a fable. Perhaps
he envied what light hit upon their sleeping; maybe
he thought a bodiless love best, unskinned

& sinless wanted to thin & glimmer like a god,
to danae and ganymede the boys with gilt & gold;
& o to finally gift with light the walls of his own

boy's room—the sorrow of all beginning—
& by which midnight gibbous did his pulse
well up, his mind struggle, tug a crucial remove

from image the way fresh milk's skimmed of skin:

tremulous

to see his boy lit up like that, cock's curve of warm
carved wax, ah—white, white, to leave himself

to that candor, that motherless suckling: what milk
there was was stanch, was salt, perhaps was love
after all, if the boy had believed a god above him, if

a man could live with a vision, divinity, & also touch it.
Hereafter, the story solely hearsay—by his own hand
his own boy hurt, dead & buried in the wood. Soon

25

rumor followed (suicide) & their double ghosts forever
kept confined to pine forest: sad, uncanny boy shadowed
by a dog he fears. This was a county in Alabama where

all your life a dead boy slept among the pines, unbroken
miles where older boys built lean-tos; come summer
Sundays, they'd stash porn mags, jack-off into yellowy rags.

Outside, your older brother's among their guns, parallel
barrels leaned into slant light: you were a body unnumbered
among them, unoriginal gunmetal, safety still ever-latched.

Afternoons, self unsignifying, you gathered the burst
blue bouquets of jays the boy left miles behind, buried
the rusted buckshot of their eyes, though the lice stunned

among blood & spine & split quills terrified as evening crept
down from the trees & the forest thickened its apparitions:
licks of white skin flickered between far-off branches, strips

lit up shirtless, fluorescent, silent as boys slipped quick between
trunks in black pantomime of catch-as-catch-can: oldest
among them, your brother, not a boy at all, shouldered his gun

like a hunter looking to hurry you home—to him kneeling
outside the bathroom door, whispering outside the bedroom
door, all the locks you turn not keeping his voice outside, all

the doors you lock not keeping him from picking the locks, him
kneeling beside the bed & not keeping his voice outside you
kneeling not keeping his body outside you so that somewhere

you're a child forever closing a door, a child forever turning
a lock—& down beneath kudzu you dug & hid & god willing
even god would never find you: all your life the dead boy

meanwhile slept: evidence: it was said among them in those parts
        a child can know too much: can die.

The Dead Boy to the Scholars
in the Library of the Fairy Tale:

"**A**t the edge of the glade
     where flanks of felled deer fade,

   there I lie, defy description, lush
        dun, antique sepia, husk, my tongue

   the cusp of damage vanishing,
        & I would touch now nothing

   but you, evidence as I am
        of imagination's end in the flesh.

   You will have to sing. Paper
        won't hold the wound I leave—"]

II.

—The Tutelary Forest

Dear Reader:

      Like a child beware & enter here beneath what branches, what waits, what watches: in the Library of the Fairy Tale a book opens to a story many more brave than you have entered, & you are in it, you are here to learn, to die, & this is how a witch gets business.

      Even though the Good Woodsman cuts the heart from a boor instead, even though to the Queen he brings it still hot in a mahogany box, she asked for yours. Any path leads to the Wolf, the Witch, the house or cottage where what waits is patient & sharp. Already, the Wolf wears the Old Woman's nightgown—his teeth white as the insides of the whitest thighs, ah—that is what paths are for, & patience.

      Bracken, bramble, thorn, thin scratched skin, this is Schwarzwald, a drop of blood enough to scent the wind: the Queen knows her rival isn't dead. Thrice before you sleep a hundred years, bearing gifts she knocks at the cottage door: poor universal virgin, you eat the apple & sleep; prick your finger & sleep; & of luck we shall not speak because you can't fuck just anyone—"It's meant to be!" the Lucky Prince says when he stumbles upon the hothouse box, glass coffin your early bloom burns inside.

      Begin, beware, will nothing save you?: in search of a place to sleep, you discover the cottage where you lie down between the white thighs of teeth & so deeply no Good Woodsman can find you. In search of sleep?—a comb, a corset, an apple. Of sleep you discover the enchanted house, & the Witch, what she does best: hungrily. Either your life's her tithe, or there's a catch: a curse, a choice: before you answer,

      remember: she would have your heart out, & eat it too. As deep calls to deep, she asked for it by name.

—In the Library of the Fairy Tale,

they would be stupid children who asked why
their parents have left them in the forest, why

their mothers hate them, their fathers haunt
their bedsteads. Here, no one in danger waits

for salvation. Here, what hungers is lovely
cruel, is gore & gorgeous & godless. It knows

spots quickest to goad blood to bruise,
the gasp & spasm & green of smothering.

How good it is, how easy, in the forest,
where you know what waits for you

adores the horror & minutiae: small bones
shattered, the slim rim of the iris in dilation.

How good, too, to know the story will forgive
you should you kill first, as when the child

goads the Witch over the trick lip of hunger
into the furnace of her own voice & is right

to do so—how good!, how easy to act
when you know your actions will be right.

It was your doubt made your brother lucky:
you would have preferred to destroy him.

—The Aviary Hour

In memory, in the fairy tales read to you before bedtime, sleep
slowly creeps into every story though rosebushes fan & flare
powdery matchsticks around the tower where even sleep's

sleeping & only a man can bless the ending—a kiss—& begin
again:
                    In memory, the fairy tale of bedtimes, the air
of the house you dreamt in drew beneath itself its thousand

black wings & shivered, brief scintillas of its million quills brilliant.
Amid feathery livery, the Prince of the aviary glistened: beak, claw,
wing & jaw—weaponry—the air his parliament, his imagination—

blackbird, jackdaw, rook & crow—jury & jurisdiction of his law
& him impotent still amid it all: your mouth his one sure dream
of sleep. There was no tale in which it had appeared, porcelain

thin-lipped sugar-bowl, a rose at the bottom: your tongue the petal
placed to sweeten the prize. There was no prior pattern to prepare
you: the stricken Prince didn't travel far from his Kingdom; fulfilled

no impossible tasks to gauge his worth; overcame no obstacles
to arrive black famine at the garden of your sleep, O child, listen:
begin again:
                    In memory, in the fairy tale of the wedding bed,

outside the chamber where even sleep was sleeping, feathers gathered
in a crush of air—it was the nightmare of the Aviary Hour, clockless
abyss where time was a song kept choked in the throats of carrion

birds. There were no witnesses, the others dreaming in the sleep
you all slept: curse of Fathers, of Mothers: family a locked cage
of relation, children bred beneath a pestilent heaven. Your souls'

malaise of stars wept pin-holes of light in an orrery under glass.
In memory, the Aviary Hour, the Prince knelt like any husband
outside the door, like any entitled by law turned the knob, entered

you: once & once & once he put himself inside you until it was dying
to be a body & still it didn't end: a kiss & the birds that were metaphors
undressed themselves & stepped pale from vast black nacre raiments

& were boys, white skin flickering shirtless between branches catch-
as-catch-can, the forest forever this time because at last he'd come
back, shouldering his gun like a Father—Look,
                                        dead boy, did you think

he'd forget you? This is Hell. A tale's told & here remains forever kept
confined to pine forest: listen: down beneath kudzu you dug & hid & god
willing it was the end & still it didn't: this is how death became the body

of a man: down in the dirt his own boy hurt: he buried him inside you
& turned the earth so you couldn't even choose let it end god be done
with me: the butt of his gun come down the one sure mercy you could see.

The room where I was born

repeats itself like paper. Origami house, her body
begins in corners where walls kiss & blister, in dry
creases coaxed crisp with spit. The bed's corsage
pressed eidetic between the white diary of walls, caul

of confessions, let me forget: blue aphasia of wrists
folded, dark, folded, her bored lullaby a small goodbye.
Let me forget: milk's wrinkled skin, breasts like bent
fingers, nipples red as rough knuckles. Let me forget

when the labial repetitions unfold, her womb rings
like an empty tin pail. I am gone. Already. Father
nurses my gums on a stain, whiskey-dipped napkin,
& brother prepares the shunt inside his arms,

flesh isolette. In the story they tell, sleep has fingers
& children need teeth grown in liquor, the skills
to hone them. They tell me "She spat you out like a curse."
I am waiting. I will not die like this again.

❧Circa

when the split began
inside the thought; when

the idea—*family*—
turned against itself,

was it father put
his spirit in a bottle?;

or mother wished him there,
a genie in reverse?—

either way he drank
and gave his fist his wife

enough to knock her up
with lullaby: tree-top

and rock-a-bye and broken
bough: from it fell

a child unbidden. She slept
for years—he found her mouth

a house and with the child
climbed inside—for years

she dreamt and this was marriage:
her long tongue a husband.

Her mind among her child—

But surely I must fear my mother's bed?

—Sophocles, *Oedipus Rex*

Then We Were Raptured:

A Sequence

Bad like

: being girls dressed up; "Pretty," old men saying, "like your mother"; a
Sunday spent in revenge, in drugstores palming penny candy into the pockets
of our corduroy dirndls:

father had left during first snow. With the car.

Grimacing against wind, we *walked* the blocks to school, sucking the
thought like peppermint. Joy hunkered in our stomachs. A hunger too strong
to be good, it turned our mouths towards sweet for days after.

Behind the candy counters of our town, beneath widow's peaks and
pitiful goatees, old men bore his drink-jaundiced face, fat clutch of pumpkins
slumping inward toward Thanksgiving.

In the evenings his absence smelled like wet wool drying, hovered inches
from our skin as if he were about to touch. We'd air it out, open windows to
snow. Then it smelled like snow hitting the radiator,

sounded like the periodic hiss of flakes going up in steam. Far past
midnight into dream, the sound wore our shoes and with his feet, his large
regular steps, took the measure of our wood floors: andante. His gait parsed
dawn into music smaller than any we had ever heard.

Sundays we searched for his teeth in every old man's smile, slipped
licorice up our sleeves and nodded, wishing to thieve each poor facsimile of
his bite. Ice clapped in the air

above the bed like a pair of hands and the room contracted—we woke,
shoes empty. Windows open, blue curtains waving

goodbye. In the mirror we smiled, wondered what it was—what we
said?—that made mother say we had his mouth.

Marriage Elegy

Her mind left her body to walk. It wasn't her fault, her fingers

anxious at hems—threads tugged, up-tucked or pulled—worrying the
edges of her household. Just a cup to soak, trash to basket, apple cored and
uneaten. Whatever a mother is

soft through our rooms—humming.

Not to wake her, we were told.

That October night her white robe brushed past the troublesome
threshold and her breath snagged updrafts, patchy and opaque; her nightgown
knelt flush up against the garden's unturned stubble; mouth pitched to ground,
she talked for a half-hour, soil rubbed fragrant as basil against her lips. Her
slippers swathed a wide dry wake through dew and went upstairs, tucked wet
in bed.

What her walking accomplished: he left us.

Days she got anxious were birds in confinement: afternoons she took
baths and let the water's one wide hand catch her pulse—fast beak tapping to
crack a seed at wrist and neck, fast on the wing—and cage it. We learned her
body

listening at the door: for an hour or more she talked as if we weren't
there.

Flint and keen, she said, her body an untouchable blade that stropped hot
against the grain of other skin. Any touch—palm against her cheek—
winnowed her down. It is true she never touched us: each loss a sleek sharp
fever.

With the right touch, any word comes up blood. It wasn't her fault. It's
true. Her lips chose—in the garden, in the bath—

she couldn't have known every word was a knife we'd use to whittle the world down to our bones, a murder going soft in the marrow of us.

"A Family Establishment"—

painted right on the sign!

Ironic, since she'd never linger there a minute—in air spiced by rinds of smoky strung sausages—not to examine the canisters of jerky thin and brittle as vanilla beans, not to praise the bright color of a rump he's just cut and decked out, in dress behind glass. Not like we would.

Summers we took pleasure

in the unopened store's dark-stained floors, the freezer where small cuts hung in splayed clusters like orchids, and our breath, caught in frost, swung subtly among the hooks. Days up front, ladies in line tapped the toes of their flats, and drunk, he'd goad chunks of ground chuck into white paper boats, smile, wax-wraps pinking over fat pounds. Whiskey: a miracle

he never lost a digit, cutting meat and drinking. In the back, apron-pocketed flask clanging metal countertops, he'd quarter chickens, blade quick through gristle and giblet, and sing Sinatra, handsome, veins on his forearms rising shiny beneath black hair.

Then one June afternoon, sent out, we waited back among the blood-and-then-some of the cans. The botched job of her soprano nagging reached us even there. And the sad flag of his laugh raised high—sudden

silence. In the slit seam of a trash bag, bad chicken wriggled in its skin, maggots bright against black plastic. "Let's go girls,"

she said, eyes behind black sunglasses. On the ride home, on the vinyl back seat, our thighs blistered and sticky. Silence. Windows closed, hot air sickened; sight ripened behind our eyes until small mouths welled up from inside, flux and flash,

intricate seed-pearls, maggots stitched glimmer into the dark garments of our skin.

Drowned Houses

No pang or panic between the ribs. It came quick when we woke, wet
bedded in our drawers. It was, we knew, unusual:

quiet. Just blood on the sheets, our white cottons dotted.

Other girls got periods, but mother said—the usual bad pun—"You're
not grammar—you're women," hence: *menstruation*, in September of that year,
the very same minute, a Saturday.

In bed reading Yeats, she ate grapefruit and granny apples because
"Bitterness keeps a figure." The clean citrus smell plumb down to our
stomachs, we spent the day dazed: tv without eating. Father came home late
from Happy Hour, said he could smell us from the street,

the whole house drowning. Our room before bedtime, exiled, backs
turned, we examined our pleated pinks in their swollen heat, together
concluded nothing odd but how we found nothing odd. Blood had always
come with feeling—blush, cut, fleet rush beneath to bruise . . .

Mother put us to bed as usual, told us her version of "Adam's Curse":

"She got knowledge first and knew two things a man never would. That
kept him crabby and distant, and Thank God, right, cherubs? Imagine. Her
mind alone in the world; how she felt, wanting to change him, split the ache
of being made aware. Your basic sour-grapes boy-hex on Eve:

he made sure she'd feel it forever."

Children's Songs

What they wished for we wanted, too, that Christmas,

the children whose rocks and songs anointed us, "Oh House, Come Out, Oh Haunts, Come Out," sing-song ghosting porch and lawn the way we were said to have done all month.

By January, they left off gossip. Wraiths are water to dry imaginations and we were no one's long cool drink—unengaging, even as Haunts.

We had become our own dark windows then, frail, quaking in static frames—mother looking into us to check her reflection—mute, but not ghosts. Nothing could move us. Like mussels, our tongues grew fat, crammed in the clamped flesh ocean of our mouths.

It is true that before he left, November dawn spread sheer over the red trash of the front yard maple, he tried to hurt her until she died.

We remember diligence as the shape of his hands.

For her—the house—to have come out of the house, he would've had to come back more himself than alive. She said anger ran her dreams, machinery stripping gears, leaving flint ground fine behind her eyes. While she slept, he came back:

crawling across the troublesome threshold at dawn with his eyes rising bilious, two pickled eggs, wearing his black suit of razors and quills, at night the silver filaments of edges sharp.

Our silence was shell around her: kept, inscrutable surface with a roar inside.

Touch

Between us we felt nothing.

Our names ill-fit, school wool: "Girls? These ladies would like a word."
Two social workers quartered the door between blue pointed shoes, regulation
flats exceptional for their gold bows, boufed ankle high. The class stared a bad
wish at our backs;

we followed to the vice principal's office where plaster saints frowsed,
dusty, foreheads carved in clenches, ecstasies of salt and roses. The suits sat us
down, smiled, moved blue ball-points chained to clipboards a wise kid would
never trust. "We've heard you're having trouble

at home." Again smiled. One of them wore spinach around a tooth. They
wanted to help. "Would you like to tell

us about it?" We felt obliged. "Such lovely faces. May we?"

They lifted our hair, pulled it behind our ears. We had no welts to offer,
bruises like soft, exotic currency—it seems they expected it. No one ever
touched us.

"There." Smiled. "Lovely. Really." Smoothed it.

What could we afford to give away?

"Why hide behind your hair?"

Then we were Raptured.

Faith moved in next door:

an albino boy, blond like sun-shot gutter glass. Summer changed sex, long
sleeves sheathed over impossible arms, pale and slender as the cream tongues
of hothouse callas.

July hemmed a heat-wave beneath our skirts.

He smelled like his mother's clean laundry, bleached sheets on the line
after evening rain. We wanted him like we wanted our father: to see him
always turning a corner, hair bright enough in sun to make us blink the image
away afterward.

Eye-level through the locked screen-door, his kewpie lips upon inspection
brimmed bloodless against a vinegary complexion. We chafed the wax off
apple skins practicing kisses we couldn't imagine leaving our mouths.

For two weeks we picked cicada skins—fragile amber split at the spine—
off sap-dry pines until we filled the twin pickle jars we'd written his name on.
Jarred slough a kaleidoscope held to our eyes, every moon that month warped
into gold, dozens of cracked fantastics.

Apiary

Albino-white and paler still against August's hothouse fog and throb, he was the beekeeper's only boy. Allergic to bees.

His father took us to the bee-barns, hutched boxes squat in fields of grass and clover, unrolled acres of painted brass. "I always wanted girls," he said and sighed, dressed us with careful keeper's hands as if for a lunar wedding: crackling apiary veils and arm-length silver gloves shivery and odd, lamé evening oven mitts.

With a can he smoked the hives. Then the prismic amber combs, prisons auric under sun. Honey-struck bees studded us in jeweled droning clumps, poison-cut facets—"Stay still," he said, "and they won't get excited." Not a breath;

we didn't even blink. We hoped he'd take us—implacable in the bed of his truck—to his boy. Unstung and unmoved, impervious to hurt, the perfect brides.

Wind shifted the fog-weathered field. Threat smothered us, a furred swelter of legs and wings, uncountable scythe blades threshing the black-gold air. "Don't panic," he said, grabbing the can, "Wait."

Heat condensed under the greenhouse scrim of screen and gloves. Our sweat a slow wet second skin, we turned salt. Peeled in sheets. Arms, faces, thighs—*that's* how the insects entered: a dream of doubled blood stung in our veins, our bodies their black echo, a flesh rung with buzz.

Home, we closed our eyes and kept to our skins: reticulate drift, vermilion skeins of clover wound tight, intricate pollen-veined wings. . . . We opened

out across the mist-rinsed grass to his yard where evening rain drew from everything a deeper double, house rinsed black and trees ambergrised under streetlight. Quartered behind windowpanes, his image wavered on the white blinds as if he'd been traced on graph paper. Hands between, dark drones worked their cells with waxen lips: from that distance his body broke into soft boxes of gold.

"Shirley Temple for the girls,"

he said, slicking back his black widow's peak two-handed with his black plastic comb. A day's dry Vitalis crackled, cellophane static from a pack of cigarettes.

"I'm the after-school special, Sid. Visiting Hours—double the usual."

The bartender slid two shots, sepia at the rims like old film flickering. "Cheers, girls, you're free for the duration. Enjoy."

Father's 'til 5 in the empty bar. A stack of quarters each, silver tilting Babels—ten apiece. We tried. Danced. First ten on the juke, A & B sides both. Patsy Cline, Elvis, Ella, Louis Armstrong. Nina Simone

made us remember we'd invented together a memory we'd always wanted: the sound of her low vibrato a box fan in our July kitchen, red crepe streamers barely stirring the heat as we danced—five and six—for mother, dressed up for once, joking. Radio tuned to sad jazz and static. Cooking, eggs with their moony albumen, bacon in the skillet. Father shaven like a Sunday, after her a little, muss and kiss. Touching, together—as in a sepia photograph we could almost believe we'd seen—they watched us—

cheek-to-cheek on slow songs

in front of the mirrored wall where father watched. Said we looked like twins, movie stars who'd break his heart, two sisters minted from one coin, child angel and her reflection, sad sweet intangibles, sweet sweet untouch-ables . . .

"You've had enough, Ray," the bartender said.

Dangerous Kitchen

Divorce proceedings: getting mother on the cross-town bus, the only one. Two hours early to make sure—"Don't rush me, cherubs. They can't start without the wife."—bath, hat, shoes, good wool suit, matching calfskin gloves. To the curb to wait.

After she left, we changed what we could: we cleaned.

After an afternoon's eternity of lye, bleach, and scalding water that left our hands' pink peeling at the cuticles; after the green sponges doused a thousand times, our arms like derricks pumping dirt from linoleum; after the unused counters scoured, stubble like ants rinsed from sticky porcelain; after his old underwear ripped into dust-rags; after buckets—brought full from the garden-hose—boiled on the stove, and sudsy hair pulled in long sopped strings from the drains:

the white. The dangerous kitchen.

When the last bus dropped her off changed in name only, we went to bed, she to her books. But every night the week after, lights out,

we played kitchen creatures, drew high the burners' blue crowns for the dark to regale itself, donned the domestic drag of aprons and oven mitts.

We gave ourselves to the knives. On the wall

drying in a line like split fish: streetlight cloven on gleaming flanks of serration, sequins bluing in schools. *To cut*, in our hands, the bread knives split their one infinitive. Pressed against skin, left red waning crescents: months dull. We remembered every weekend father cutting nothing,

sharpening-stone moist with oil, imitated with our voices the slow high slice-slicing of the blade, back-and-forth his body against the stone a thrust almost a rocking,

a man's lullaby: mothering the blade.

II

Agoraphobia: A Reply

(*Telemachus to Penelope*)

Not yet. Frost hasn't hit. Gripping the branches, only
crabapples last, balled infants' fists, toughest parts turned
inward. No not depressed. Just sick inside all week.
Cars slur by; the windows itch in their panes, crawl
the opposite wall. I watch into drift, liquid fever-shift.
Mother, inside me the room busies your hands.

No I'm—just watchful and counting things: pills, pages
read, days until my birthday. Of course send money. Yes
no socks. No anything in bulk. Leaves, early this year,
measure the yard in hands, days in falling. I was in bed
when a man and a rake came to bargain; he gathered
a whole afternoon in a handshake and led the yard away.

Let me remind you what you taught: home, one can
claim nowhere comfortable, no place private. *That*
is why your children suffer self like heavy clothes
shrugged off when hot. Mothered things card misery
like wool, find themselves rich with this one action:
minutes. Spun into finest thread, I've never loved

anyone as I love you in my disappearing:

> in hours, the room will work me into tapestry.

Set for a Southern Gothic

> Saul told his son Jonathan and all his officials
> that he planned to kill David.
>
> —I Samuel 19:1

Because David & Jonathan

touch. After the youth, carrying arrows back to town, has gone.
In the field soft with shot bodies of birds.
    In the field that is a kiss, text made real
by rot, claw and wing, and maggots' mouths
    glossing the white lines of feather and bone. They touch

and air leaches riches from milkweed, each pod a burst
    coin purse, seeds like lambent metals spent and aloft. Touch
(youth gone, his quiver filled with feathers),
    and the father's body marks the field's edge, fear
a hard dirt road to town where skin's worn loose

like cotton cloth. Touch: the Book's page's turned,
both were crying as they kissed each other, verse declaimed
    to a congregation, 1984, field made real in Alabama,
in a church where heat of day and red clay dust
    swarmed the windows, cut and stained glass where angels edited

the text of Heaven, church where the preacher's lips erased
    the men's skin-to-skin in the boy's—*my*—mind. His childhood
lost the ruin that is their kisses, text, field where two men
    are losing each other to the white page of day, watching grass knife up

ciphers in the light, small bodies of never-again feathered
    and easy with gore in the heat. *Once again Jonathan made David promise
to love him* in the text, enough only for the shallow kiss
    of the word "friend." Their names' necessary knives skimmed his skin,
childhood desire the sinewy scar that grew over the wound

57

of their touches, his mind a book where the most someone could write
was: *better even than the love of women*: enough
    to love them like this, back-lit with the losses of history, to note
the way the preacher lip-synched, cinched lips
    that ask me still to name this kiss otherwise. Carrying arrows,

the youth—a boy himself—stops on the road back,
    wind loose in its slough of red dust, wind spreading bright seed
in a quick circumference, and the boy turns, text
    deepening in the light, two men losing the field to something

brighter, erasure, the boy's gaze taking it in, their body
    called love staked out in the grass against the historical
edge of the father's body.
    The boy I was knew the plot from here:
the field's blueprint suggests a bier

    for the beloved; the road delivers
his father's orders to march in a war
    he won't survive; and never was anyone so much a coward
as David now, silent even beneath the oath
    of kisses, among the grasses who make a pleasant measure of rot

and heat as they pitch song against themselves,
    this King who will sing so well of love only after his lover is dead.
The boy witnessed the preacher allow Jonathan to say

    The Lord will make sure that you and I,
and your descendents and mine, will forever keep
    the sacred promise we have made each other,

and he feared the preacher could make the Lord
    make sure of anything, say anything in that church
wearing the red cotton shroud of dust loose
    in summer air, in that stifled heaven where angels enumerated
the blessed on lists rich with editing,
    and the boy thought he knew already—

pressed hot on the pew between mother's thigh and father's elbow—
    how a secret skin's worn tight as summer behind the knees.

But he couldn't see this silence only begins

    the story, the long one the preacher made the Lord name
sinful, where two men lose themselves forever
    to something brighter in a field whose air bristles static
with the electricity of seed, where the only road out is death.

    Fear marked the beginning of the father's body in me:

there is no road out of the body they make in the field.

                                  (*for Jim Elledge*)

Trick Noir

Close your eyes and you're stoned, child, here on River Road
where the city on the banks begins, fished quick like river-trash
up from the water. Imagine. Follow the water-silt and stink,

valley laid out ribboning black and fog-licked up hills
from the riverbed. Imagine wet asphalt wheezing beneath tires
as he drives, gin-bottle rattling on the floor. Sitting shotgun,

you're stoned. Don't panic—grin at his jokes. Try not to think:
the minister's too-sweet son, locker-room jocks, Daddy's .38,
or the girlfriend you can't get it up for. You're sixteen, sweet

Jesus, don't you get it?—his fingers easing up the cuff of your
shorts, curving in over your thigh—he's married. Imagine
the cool metal as he says *Nice—is this for me?* and, go ahead,

what stoned boy wouldn't smile, first-time high and happy
he's hard for once? He's not handsome, this man, not anyone
you'd want to see again but you will: he's got a truck and a place

to fuck, and that's what the city likes, wheels and sex between men
discreet. Open your eyes. Roadside trailers laid out end-to-end
repeat like railcars in the rain. Could be your life, his, imagine—

scrub pines leak sap into the truck-bed. The white detonations
of oncoming cars etch error into each windshield-streak, play up
the fracture inherent in glass. Believe me, in time you'll look back

on these moments when you're drunk or stoned and he's taking you
back to his place where he'll pay you after, but not yet, no, now,
please, forgive yourself of the future—of his hand; of the ring bright

on his finger; of the river moaning in pine-wet wind; of velocity;
of how you'll bend in his bed; of the honkey exotic in his gold-tooth
smile; of moist dark green bills; of the need they'll leave behind—

and I too will forgive you, briefly, here where the city's beauty begins
by touching you. The day he asks *It's our secret?* you'll swear *Yes* to him
and ten others just like him and it will never stop again, touch.

As for me, I'm no one you know; I exist only in future tense.
Don't imagine me, please, there where you are, hard beneath
a stranger's hands. Close your eyes. The wind is thick, awake

where the kudzu chokes the creekbeds that follow the road.
Listen: know that I think of you and the city, its green river-
stink, black asphalt giving rise to mist at the rank apex of evening.

All beauty, its excess and rot, begins here, at the end of River Road
where the city slides its lights into water slow beneath the bridge,
and there's beauty, too, in the tinny chuckle of his belt unbuckling,

in the crushed corsage his underwear makes on the floor,
in the tick of bills he counts out after. Remember it's the same
for us all: you wouldn't believe the life you'll be asked to live.

For seven months of tenth grade you'll feel stubble burning,
bruises pitted black from skin like cherry-stones, pinched nerves
singing against school desks and your mind lost to knowledge

because the city's secret touches you all day and no one can know.
Each algebraic equation halved by his having you, metaphor
a vehicle—its engine idles in your mind—imagine the distractions

of geography: by night the city'll spread himself out on greasy sheets
creased like a map where his cock is compass—rose, and risen,
dizzy with fixity—and his mechanic's hands engineer the scale

on which you're laid. His lessons will teach you this much:
there are only two ways to fuck a boy and be a man—drunk,
or paying for it—and anything else, he'll say, is less than a man

and worse than a woman: a faggot. Which would be you.

Against Abstraction

If I had what you might call a "heart," it'd be junk
cars, antique trash whose back seats we fucked in, vinyl

split by weather and nesting, mouse piss in winter.
Trick's kisses were old Marlboros, tight-rolled joints:

dry, careless heat, tobacco or flint. Smoke finished,
"Damn, I'm pissed," he—whoever—would say,

with a flick of tongue or wrist. Really, my heart's
the old joke about men and their blood: enough only

for one organ at a time. "Love" was rough
trade unshaved, fake name washed off at home.

Stoned, each one thought there was no worth
in what a man couldn't touch or buy with skin,

thought the same of a man who'd let him: fifteen bucks
a pop, stud unknuckled with a one-handed kiss. Head

back, he'd proclaim the roof's frayed fabric beautiful.
"Jesus!" he'd say—never my name—knees

foxing my ears in the breathless beneath of a sky
never sky, that classic starless economy: empty.

Set for a Southern Gothic

From here, this poem a neon pall over the tarry asphalt,
it's too cliché to be sympathetic, really, the black Caddy
the boy spills out of in stacked heels and hot-pants, the man
plump in the word *seersucker*—suit, straw hat, white oxfords—
the boy—it's sad—young enough to think such a get-up
original. If I had to, I'd start with the motel before they screw
everything up, the boy and his "companion." Or maybe
the sign, *Moon-Winx*, ironic only for its regulars who joke,
Girl, *shit*—even the Man-in-the-Moon has to turn a trick.
Sure as hell ain't no shut-eye going on in there.

✳

"It's hot," I could start, "It's 1989." But it's only Alabama,
July, a town where *this time* the man hasn't worn underwear;
he's wearing too much cologne. This time, he's nervous.
The boy snaps grape Bubblicious. Trouble with the key,
the man's palms swampy—bad sign. The boy checks
his memory in the shine on the car's hood: yep, he *is* cute.
From his jacket pocket, the man takes a silver flask flashy
as a sports car, drags a deep draught. Sets to work again,
jimmying the door. It gives like a sigh. It startles them both.

✳

                              I'd start with anything
but what they have, that room's air, interior scrubbed raw
with the smell of sex, accordion noise of the overtaxed a/c,
mildew filming the bathroom with spoor, I'd give them
anywhere else. Start five months back when they meet
at a bar, boy starry-eyed with poppers, man sleek with liquor,
the Dollar Inn after. Start at the Moon-Winx in March
April May June, the scandal of the boy's oral precocity,

the man's wedding band, how they make "missionary"
an anachronism. The bills in the boy's back pocket as he leaves.

✖

What in this cheap scenery is equal to what they have? There
a cigarette burns, improbable, propped on the busted tv;
burn marks blossom on the bed-sheets instead of flowers;
the ashtray clots with offal. I'd like a better set, words
to help pretend it's not rank as ever in here, but the boy too
knows oily condoms coil in on themselves, spent beneath
the unmade bed. What can I say? The boy likes the idea, fucking
in someone else's filth, but the man opts for some dignity
tonight: they'll do it in the shower instead.

✖

I don't want it at all, not again, not
this 4th of July, not this boy who skipped family fireworks
spitting his gum into the ashtray, this man who made excuses
to miss the fiftieth annual Episcopal picnic slipping his jacket
onto the one wire hanger by the door. Don't want the man
unknotting his tie, the boy sucking in his stomach before
the mirror warped with water. But it all happens anyway,
the man behind, the kisses he gives so careful, complex
and timid, the boy's confused. He only understands how
to play war, siege that opens its fields in trick affection,
all subterfuge and foreplay, I watch it start in him, beloved
tripwire skin—

it's what he feels best. Has to think of it this way
to feel anything at all.

✖

There's a way the room looks
before the man sets it loose (the ending I don't have to make),
a way memory retouches the tawdry with compassion: the man
maudlin and soft with drink (graying, if you hadn't guessed—

his daughter's a year behind the boy in school); the boy naked
and angry with pleasure, his body's betrayal. They look hopeful
maybe, unpunished, but for certain there's a moment fraught
with grace, the whole room getting lucky, the air ragged
with kisses before the man whispers into the boy's neck his mistake
(the moment I would give up to change), before the man, bent
over the boy's neck, lets go the slip always in check, words
unsheathing the knife in his voice, shucking its shiver deep
in the flesh, and how do I know it isn't—

                                        "I love you," he says.

❧ Circa

and I the child who's two of everything/ first father

> *leave child and never back. into the field disappear and never*

second father/ the first smiles while the second

> *stop. the photographs cannot follow beneath skin. and never*

wets the lips beneath his skin/ he is first mother under

> *back to the house. beneath your skin disappear and never*

his tongue/ he hides her nipples and milks the two skins

> *follow into the child beneath the house. and stop and never*

between mothers with the knowledge she is half

> *house the photographs in skin. into the never back and never*

father between her legs and second again inside/

> *you can never leave the photographs and disappear.*

his voice parts her lips/ and whose voice now is mine

> *you can never leave the photographs and disappear.*

But the body, I suppose, like a lump of coal, fulfills its highest function when it is being consumed.

—H.D., Notes on Thought and Vision

The Word Cock & the Sublime

Detail from "Set
for a Southern Gothic"

On the spread the boy unbuckles like an old leather belt.
Burn marks blossom on the bed-sheets instead of flowers.

A last long swallow and the man caps his flask. I come back
to this, how the boy knows the man feels whiskey secure

a door behind which his wife and daughter sleep. The way
he lights a cigarette and laughs (crack of the glass ashtray

smacked down) when the man asks, "Aren't you too young
to smoke?"
     Now I will say it: the boy *does* think about the word

"love," wonders if what he feels (hot ash flaring at the cherry)
as the man's pants tent, is that something like it? The man undoes

his shirt's pearled buttons (fingertips square, nails cleaned
and clipped) down to the slight furred swell above his belt

where the boy knows the man will guide his head. I could tell you
what I once thought lead the boy here, but I'm not sure I believe

the clear theorems now, in this room again: can I say "victim"
as the man's pants unzip, "perpetrator," as the boy kneels

at the bed's edge? I permit, now, the sound of one word only: *Power*.

◼

Forgive me—it's how I feel best, how I have to think about it
to feel anything at all. Isn't it easier if *The boy unbuckles on the spread*?

73

If *The man undoes his shirt's pearled buttons*? If "power" is the sole word
the boy can own? I didn't want to make it difficult, but: the sink

dingy where he spit out the cum, three of four condoms they'll leave
in the trash, the ashtray's clotted offal, the man sobbing *please, please*

into the boy's arched back, the ribs whose curl his fingers follow into
as if into touch-closed mimosa leaves, don't you see how the plot turns

on the word "love"? The boy's vertebrae unbuckle in the man's hands,
the angle of the last sweet thrust. And the man empearling his back, *please*

please, arias cramped and final in the throat, the thick sweet salt-reek
rich in air and on skin. The boy, his cinched mouth a flat-line of pleasure.

✖

Where I love the man, this moment, I never expected to.
Here, as the neon *Moon-Winx* sign draws its appalling wash

over the scene, Man-in-the-Moon winking as if anything
might be bought for the price of a room, in this mean

blue light of memory, I'm able to love the leathery stretch
of the man's testicles, the vulnerable little cinch between,

the rings seaming his bent neck, the silver filaments he's proud of
wiring his temples and chest, the hard square reach of his thumbs,

and as the boy gets up to wash himself, as the man lights
the story's familiar post-coital smoke, as the man waits, watches

steam steal into itself, rain-sound roiling from beneath the door,
I allow the sound of only one other word: *Expense*. "I love you,"

the man says, *VACANCY* the light his skin blues beneath,
and how does the boy know it isn't true as he counts greenbacks

in his head, distance, how close to New York they could get him . . .

74

Water corrects the errors, softens the small smeared pears, bruise-
prints picked one and one and one from his ribs. When he breathes,

the ribbed pears swell and beat against their skins, seconds until
their noise subsides back into blood. His breath catches at the man's touch

(he didn't hear—) and his mind, a child's room shaped by the sound
of rain, dissipates as the man enters him. The boy starts down the long

thin hallway of sex, and I follow, naked linoleum echoing. On the walls,
the bulbs' lumens pin flickering shadows like wings of caught birds—bare

bulbs and bent wire cages, pale blue walls lined with barred windows
where men stare and stroke the dark towards an ecstasy of salt. No one

is safe. Not here. Not the boy who walks always toward the ending
I no longer have to make, not the man as he hastens over the vacancy

of his labor. I use the men who watch and stroke the dark to measure
the distance between us; they are the price of that distance: with each one

he was the door to a room shaped by the sound of rain, and each one
was for a little while the applause of water on a tin roof: with each

he could briefly think: I'm beneath summer rain; I've never been touched.

House in Summer
with a Slapped Face in It

Again: he swears he'll never. Smiles
    as if he will. Outside, the tulip tree
        fills out its form in triplicate: pink, discreet. Deliberate trickery,

he pins your palm on your favorite
    of his shirts, and beneath, his heart,
        tiny needle's eye, conducts its study of an endless thread

of blood: *Cross my heart and hope . . .*
    he says. And winks. Outside, spring wizens
        on the stem, slumps its crippled wilts toward summer. And swears

he'd swear even on the cracked back
    of his mama's fat Bible, spine split
        by goldleaf, swears he hopes he'd want to. Never (your hand

at the dropped stitch of his pulse),
    not again. From where you stand,
        never's not far off: in summer, a closed house grows toward it,

a wilderness: in the bedroom, he strips. You
    are like the roses, confuse thorn and bloom,
        who is rack and who is screw. . . . After, in the rusty tub, he draws you

a bath amber with sap; he cleans you sleepless
    with the usual question: in the kitchen, in the sink,
        a ruin of crows rings, black telephones. Who'd answer if you'd leave?

Tenement Body

The air swells—pure burn; the windows sweat.
Among a stale scatter of bread, I wait for birds.

The sexual rope of wisteria on the arbor:
since leaving, I conjure what he thinks, writes

about me in letters never sent: *The flare of your*
fine flanks I can do without, but your mouth I miss,

your palate's vellum. Now a cardinal—plumage
a wound I won't write down to send him.

Summer air frank with fever, the blooms' reek
burns. Were I to go home, let his hands collage

my flesh, graft the blistering nipples to air . . .
I memorized the orchard of your sleep, I wrote,

the breath's found wet feather; the slick windfall
skin; its rich, bruised smell. Him an orchard

because things are easier to leave. More quaint
the token bruises of fallen fruit than the bird

wearing loud violence like a gown. Whose
tongue would submit, to artifice, the mouth?

The body is its own convict. Yes. He would invent me
again, screw my heart's charge in hard. Leave me

as I left him: weathering the tenement body.
Combing the cold barbecue for bread,

the cardinal catches—thrall—its feathers
a thrill of combustion, its wings awash in ash.

The Word *Cock* & the Sublime

Memory of him begins in my mouth; finger whet

red with Chianti, slicked around the rim of a glass half-full
slips a harmonic: sere, sweet vibration a cricket would make
if it could sustain its dumb broken one-note.

Porch: evening low-slung from telephone wires.
Wine on my finger, put to lips: a way of thinking
that begins in the mouth. Because when I say it
it is both the thing and not the thing
                              you can't say
the word without the throat opening of its own accord—*ä*—
ache just now, just a little past the tongue's work—*k*—cut,
thrust forward in the mouth, can't think without tasting saliva.

Maudlin now, ridiculous tippler of awful Chianti—his favorite—
I find myself mouthing—short fat shock of it—practicing,
word that opens and closes around nothing in the mouth,
                              needs no articulate tongue
and no teeth but breath.
                    Undressed, he was a thousand metaphors,
anything but flesh the quality of light within his skin, a sheen
both supple and subtly stubbled—like thick handmade paper—

it held its own shadow.
                    Undressed, a thousand metaphors
for loss, the way I realized a room holds two bodies
differently than one
                    only after he'd gone, a certain gracious angle
of the interrupted cigarette forgotten in the ashtray, a solicitousness
in the light's awkward fall down his back, dizzying splay of angles.

He loved to make me beg, say the word I blushed to say—ripe-tipped plum
teased on the tongue—because it's bad
to want it and even worse to put it in your mouth,
both the thing and not the thing, and each time when finally he'd fuck me

all words were hands, each syllable a finger pulling thought taut as a sheet
and I understood how sudden language can die
in the body, the locked dark box of the throat the emptiest pleasure:

how a mouth can open and close on nothing.

—of a Sleeping Man,
& a Second Man Awake

(for John Wieners, 1934–2002)

So love unhoused us: sweat
the summer's continual
    hotel, we left skin
        through doors of white rime, left

    what had been made, unmade—
sheets the bleach of paregoric
    behind the eyes.
        Image: our silver skin filled,

    copper from inside out . . .
But could taste the needle—
    the pain of sleep
        in a cheap room—could taste

    the cradle of the vein: unguent
a lullaby for comfort
    and phosphorous,
        blue, hush a flame starving air

    of oxygen. Chemistry:
what drew likeness
    to our minds . . .
        Had never made fists like these—

    syringe's sudden jump of blood;
never heard dilations
    sheet silence whitely
        over everything; the heart—raw

nautilus—seal, receding, each breath
in chambers one
    by one closer, taut
        to the esophagal knot; love

    unhoused us thus: saw: our slapped skin
rise iodine, rose-
    gold before the light;
        mercuric trembling over the treble

    descant of flame; a solution, we thought,
a fix of image
    to self, perpetual hotel.
        Daguerreotype: of a sleeping man,

    and a second awake: I remember him and again
we're material
    for light to write on,
        most fragile of mediums—

    a breath could wreck it—

Then David left, and Jonathan went back to the town.

—I Samuel, 20:42

Toward Lost Letters

Toward Lost Letters

7/21

Dear Ernst Krieger:

       The photo album unfolds its aerial cemetery
map. From each snapshot's plot, dust escapes the cracked felt black
in which my mother keeps your effigy: in a greenhouse among roses,
you smile, shears cutting a smear of light across the frame.

       My lover says I look like you, same shy height
pushing the same round shoulders forward, short hair curling
in humid air. It's a fact mother's always claimed: I'm her only child
to take after you—

       a similar *way* about us. Quiet, bookish—"You *know*."
I can guess what she means. The rest is official by document: born 1899,
Alsace-Lorraine, German Catholic, last of eleven, the baby. 1919: immigrated
with your sister, my grandmother. A horticulturist, never married. American
for fifty-odd years. It is, all of it, official:

       a year after my birth, dead
by your own hand. Age: seventy-six—no note. And this

       one photograph—

   ✖

All my life I've remained the student
who "thinks *feelingly*," a professor once wrote, whose "passion
and discourse err on the inaccurate," meaning: "Have you *heard*
of Plato?" As a lover, my discourse hasn't improved. E.g.:

the man I'm seeing has gold in his mouth,
likes sex out loud. First time in bed, he said "Better be careful.
I'm a screamer"—New York native, he's a sweet butch Mama's boy
from the Bronx, can't imagine anywhere without Chinese laundries,
prostitutes and ACT UP nuns—but I stayed quiet

about Baptist fish fries, kudzu, peanut boils,
the Boll Weevil festival. About times I got stopped at the high school doors,
boys wanting to hear me say "I'm a faggot," who had to know how much
I wanted to suck them off before I could go inside and learn what else
there was to learn.

It's too easy to say they wanted to hear
what they themselves couldn't say. I thought they wanted
to hear they would always have youth and power, the cruelty
of their fathers' work boots. I thought he didn't understand
what it meant, years of "*Shhh*, someone might hear," fear
a man's hand across my mouth. Meaning someone might hear
something he couldn't lie about later:

I can't calculate the price on our mouths.

Last week we went to a panel about "Queer
Language." The panelists argued: homosexuals didn't exist
"as we know them" until Victorians coined the word; or Stonewall,
something about a common culture—Judy Garland, hankie codes,
poppers. The man I'm seeing said bull—the Greeks were pretty okay.
I thought: no one word is culture enough, and: homosexuals "*as we
know them*"?—I'm not convinced. My mother, for example, that coded *way*

we have of being similar; my boyfriend I thought
never silenced, whose father—I learned—threw him out on the street

at sixteen, whose mother refuses calls and letters; and you, in this absence
you left, I'm inventing assent, inheritance and common traits, desires,
the word *Expense*. If I'm wrong, tell me—it must mean something

              that I choose silence with a man whose gold mouth
moves me, so hard to believe

              when he says I'm safe, here: no one is listening—

              Am I right? I think now that error is the feeling.

✠

I can't imagine the courage it took to touch him.

When mother told me she remembers you went
to college in Mannheim, I'd already invented him, your young seminarian—
feverish, fresh from reading Augustine—looking for sins to complicate his faith;
and how, at first, thoughtless hours with you filled the time left unscheduled
from vespers to compline, all the unnamed offices of ordinary time, altars
made at night of the body . . .

Black triumvirate—silence, death, dirt—I think

of him often—your Berndt? Stefan?—how you met
that day swimming. I almost remember the slope of his neck, nape
where it met back, how your fingers hurt to map the small topography
of topmost vertebrae, the wet descension of spine. And what of the days
that followed, the way your shoulders seemed

always about to brush?

He left you for the Church, of course, or: you left
too soon for America, country where all touches stop. Fifty years' sweet favorite
uncle of every remembered girlhood, photogenic fop, you cultivated a manner
sexless as your blue-ribbon roses: a naturalized citizen. Aloof, eunuch's smile
a corsage of such pale pink the petals look white—hothouse hybrid you bred
for a decade to get the pink flesh bleached to a fade.

The photograph shows how, in the damp light
of the greenhouse, your mouth takes its place among the work of a lifetime.
How your hands, soft with the shears, cut only blooms perfect for Sunday table.

✖

I've decided—he wrote you—imagined:

       ink in softest envelopes; every month crisp oily onionskin
fragile at folds where his tongue made creases pliable; script thin where the nib
began to run dry; the upswept blue where you hoped he cried, pressed his lips.

       He wrote how he was wrong, of course. How he missed
your body—what he remembered best—your flaws: the slight bowed, webbed
toes . . .

       Sometimes in this new town I forget the words—you wrote.

       I think of you in Indianapolis, worrying new English
like a rosary, plying its mysteries. Each syllable crystalline with its own amen,
each word a common prayer. It must've been necessary amnesia, a new language
almost a *body*,

       a faith large enough to hold God again.

       After his first letter—did you know that no word
in any language could save you? You were already dead. You left him
as testament, your only personal document, the text of your death, the last
absent note: his body, equal history of alphabet and suicide, body of love-
letters burnt, body of your lover buried, I write over oceans and find your desire
speechless. . . . Yet,

       there was a way money dropped in the votive box brought
him closer, votives breathing like wine in their red cups, a penny per match
so you could kneel again near heat.

    ✗

In bed tonight, we had our usual historical argument:

what is it two bodies make of each other?

Not Aristophanes' monadic romance, he said, not the one
body separated by gods: give me a break. When I showed him these letters,
he said my desires were laughable, my ideas cruel, that I condemned *you* instead
of the limits of history. What I couldn't say to him then, I will say now:

just as our two bodies do not become one, but a third
whose flesh I can't understand, I have hoped for you a body that seems at first
improbable.

There must be another body—history's—and I want this,
our third, to have lived, to have written a common book of letter and flesh
whose paper is wet, sewn with salt, its type set with ink and sweat. Do you see?
I want its first word to be *Yes*.

What I'm trying to say is:

in your small rented room in Mannheim, history stopped,

your mouth one among the folds and roseate furrows
of him, musk pungent up under your nails, spit christening the work of each
crease and underthing; your mouth between cock and asshole, the fine thick
perineal seam, the sodomy your tongue ran up,

I say history stopped—

And the body of history begins again here: mouth between,
hands between, words split

and tongue, scent fast on these letters—

I write out loud your sexed and crowded mouth.

Yours, Ever,

B—

Circa

But this is years later—a county field dreamy with weeds:

high grass and sheaves of chamois-
          soft air polished themselves until music
                    fell out minutiae: trinkets, plinks. What hurdy-gurdy, what

operetta, crickets and cicadas, frogs,
          boxy aria of insects turned with a crank.
                    There a boy on the bank made counterpoint in his head,

river-rift where minnows sifted shadow
          from shallows, current turning
                    the enviable stones, each thin pocked rind perfect in mind

for skipping distance. When light hit
          the river and the world's double hung
                    upside-down and ripples rung from inside it like a bell;

when his mother a mile away beat air
          into copper again with a stick
                    and supper pot and her one song scanning iambs—*come*

home come home come home—; when
          he thought *home*: it was a decision;
                    it was physical; it was a wish:

                              a boy slipped the skin

of the literal until there was no house
          could hold him, *goodbye*. Somewhere
                    in the real, someone—a double, a liar—was running home.

95

Notes

"After the thorns I came to the first page," is from Randall Jarrell's poem, "The Sleeping Beauty: Variation of the Prince," which can be found in *The Seven-League Crutches* (New York: Harcourt, Brace and Company, 1951).

✶

"Rules for the Telling" owes a debt of imagery and metaphor to Randall Jarrell's "La Belle au Bois Dormant," also in *The Seven-League Crutches*.

✶

"Sleeping Beauty & the Prince: Self-portrait as Victim & Perpetrator" also owes much to Jarrell's poem "The Sleeping Beauty: Variation of the Prince." The italicized passages consist of names of rose breeds, while the meanings behind various formations, colors, and states of maturity of roses are borrowed from a florist's dictionary, now lost.

✶

"Begin, Beware—" owes limitless debts—borrowings and other inspiration—to other texts, and those whose influence I can consciously remember and thus honor here are these: Bruno Bettelheim, *The Uses of Enchantment: The Meaning and Importance of Fairy Tales* (New York: Alfred A. Knopf, 1976); Cathy Caruth, *Unclaimed Experience: Trauma, Narrative, and History* (Baltimore: Johns Hopkins University Press, 1996); Brothers Grimm, *The Complete Fairy Tales of the Brothers Grimm*, trans. Jack Zipes (New York: Bantam Books, 1987); Susan Howe, *My Emily Dickinson* (Berkeley: North Atlantic Books, 1985); Randall Jarrell, *The Complete Poems* (New York: Farrar, Straus & Giroux, 1969); Carolyn Kay Steedman, *Landscape for a Good Woman: A Story of Two Lives*. (New Brunswick: Rutgers University Press, 1987); Stith Thompson, *The Folktale* (Berkeley: University of California Press, 1977) and *Motif-Index of Folk Literature: A Classification of Narrative Elements in Folk Tales . . .,*6 vols. (Bloomington: Indiana University Studies, 1926–32); Marina Warner, *From the Beast to the Blonde* (New York: Farrar, Straus and Giroux, 1995); and Jack Zipes, *Fairy Tales and the Art of Subversion* (New York: Routledge, 1991).

✶

The final line of "Agoraphobia: A Reply" owes a great deal of its phrasing to the penultimate lines of Deborah Digges's poem "Spring," from *Rough Music* (New York: Alfred A. Knopf, 1995).

✖

"—of a Sleeping Man, and a Second Awake" owes inspiration and imagery to the life and writings of the poet John Wieners, especially to the volumes *The Hotel Wentley Poems* (original versions) (San Francisco: David Haselwood, 1965); *Ace of Pentacles* (New York: James F. Carr & Robert A Wilson, 1964); and *The Journal of John Wieners is to be called 707 Scott Street for Billie Holiday 1959* (Los Angeles: Sun and Moon Press, 1996). Additionally, much of the poem's description is borrowed from technical terminology—the construction of the daguerreotype plate and the chemical process of creating an image upon it—found in Aaron Scharf's *Pioneers of Photography* (New York: Harry N. Abrams, Inc., 1976). It was written in memory of Wieners.

✖

"Toward Lost Letters": The poem's inception lies in Cixous' *Three Steps on the Ladder of Writing* (New York: Columbia University Press, 1993).—"I said that the dead are our first masters, those who unlock the door for us that opens onto the other side, if only we are willing to bear it. Writing, in its noblest function, is the attempt to unerase, to unearth. . . ."